CREEPY CHRONICLES

Maniacal Monsters and Bizarre Beasts

Written by Barbara Cox and Scott Forbes

Gareth Stevens
Publishing

CONTENTS

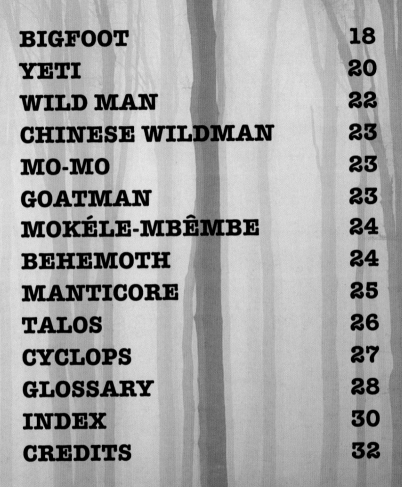

Werewolves, mummies, and monsters, oh my! We love to see these terrifying creatures in movies, but what if you ran into one? Not possible? Are you sure?

Bigfoot's footprints have been seen by many, mummified bodies can be found all over the world, and werewolves return to human form during the day, so who really knows? The safest thing to do is avoid mountains, tombs, swamps, deserts, forests, fields, and especially being outside during a full moon. Maybe it would be best if you just stayed inside.

MANIACAL
MONSTERS
AND
BIZARRE
BEASTS

WEREWOLF

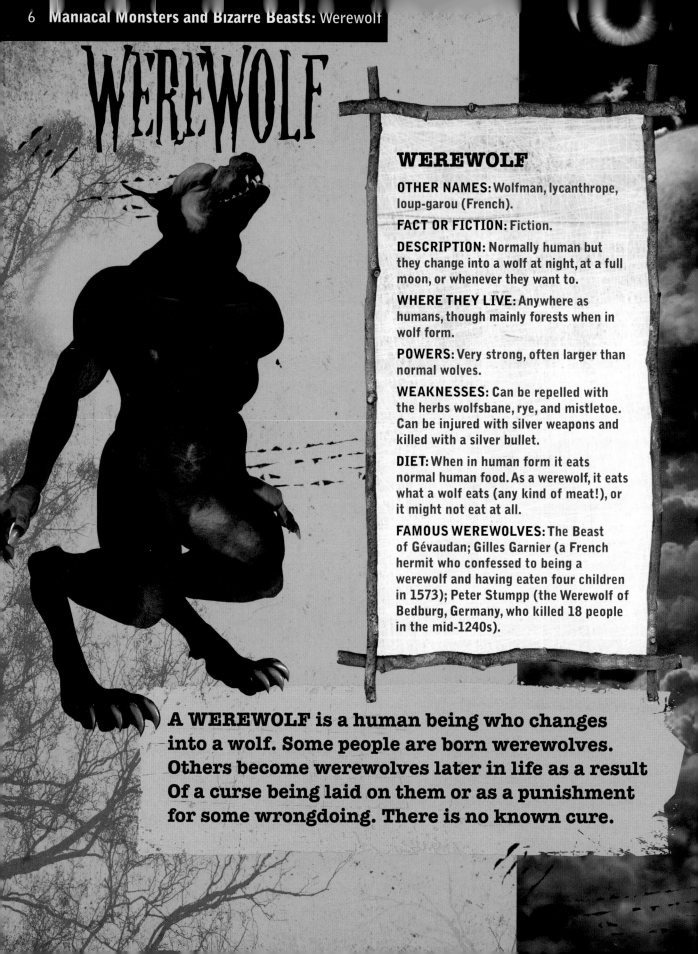

WEREWOLF

OTHER NAMES: Wolfman, lycanthrope, loup-garou (French).

FACT OR FICTION: Fiction.

DESCRIPTION: Normally human but they change into a wolf at night, at a full moon, or whenever they want to.

WHERE THEY LIVE: Anywhere as humans, though mainly forests when in wolf form.

POWERS: Very strong, often larger than normal wolves.

WEAKNESSES: Can be repelled with the herbs wolfsbane, rye, and mistletoe. Can be injured with silver weapons and killed with a silver bullet.

DIET: When in human form it eats normal human food. As a werewolf, it eats what a wolf eats (any kind of meat!), or it might not eat at all.

FAMOUS WEREWOLVES: The Beast of Gévaudan; Gilles Garnier (a French hermit who confessed to being a werewolf and having eaten four children in 1573); Peter Stumpp (the Werewolf of Bedburg, Germany, who killed 18 people in the mid-1240s).

A WEREWOLF is a human being who changes into a wolf. Some people are born werewolves. Others become werewolves later in life as a result of a curse being laid on them or as a punishment for some wrongdoing. There is no known cure.

CURSE OF THE WEREWOLF

There are a few theories as to why people become werewolves. Two sure-fire ways are to be bitten by a werewolf or to be cursed by a sorcerer. Some people choose to become werewolves and rub a magic ointment on themselves or put on a bewitched wolfskin belt in order to transform. A few other rather unpleasant ways are to drink the rainwater that gathers in the footprint of a werewolf or to drink water from a cup fashioned from the skull of a werewolf.

THE WEREWOLF LOOK

Werewolves turn into wolves at night and are usually bigger and fiercer than a real wolf, with red, glowing eyes. They may run on all fours or walk on two legs. Either way, they are horrifying since they spend most of their time using their huge claws and fangs to attack and devour animals, people, and even bodies from graveyards.

By day, however, a werewolf will normally return to human form and may appear quite normal—aside from some telltale signs. If you suspect someone of being a werewolf, check whether they display any of the following—eyebrows that meet in the middle, particularly hairy skin or hairy palms, pointed ears, a stumpy tail, unpleasant body odor, or a dislike of bright light. If so, be on your guard. Another sign is hair inside the skin, but that's harder to check!

BY THE LIGHT OF THE MOON

Some werewolves can change into a wolf whenever they wish. Others have no control over their condition and may find themselves turning into a wolf every time darkness falls, or, more usually, whenever there is a full moon. Often the werewolf will wake in human form the next day, with no recollection of the awful things they have done.

THE BEAST OF GÉVAUDAN

Between 1718 and 1721, the village of Gévaudan in central France was terrorized and more than 100 people were said to have been killed by a huge wolflike beast that walked on two legs. The French king sent troops to hunt the beast and eventually it was killed. Descriptions of its body vary, but it was said to be very strange and have small ears and hoof-like feet.

Above: The Beast of Gévaudan.

THEY'RE EVERYWHERE!

Stories of werewolves come from all over the world and date back thousands of years. In ancient Greece, wolfmen were mythical figures associated with the gods and there were shrines and cults devoted to them. Ancient Romans believed that magic spells and herbs could turn a person into a wolf— a "versipellis" or "turnskin," they called it. In eighth-century Iraq, scholars reported that wolflike monsters killed hundreds of people and stole children from their beds.

By the Middle Ages, belief in werewolves was widespread in Europe, but people had come to think of them as the servants of the Devil. So, werewolves were greatly feared and people with wolflike tendencies were persecuted. This was particularly the case in sixteenth-century France, where suspected werewolves were regularly burned alive.

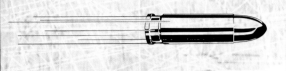

STOPPED IN ITS TRACKS?

A silver bullet can stop a werewolf in its tracks and even kill it, but that might not be the end of your troubles. It is said that unless their bodies are burned, werewolves return to life—as vampires!

NAVAJO SKINWALKER

In the southwestern United States, people don't just turn into wolves but also coyotes, bears, cougars, and foxes. The people in question are Navajo Skinwalkers, medicine men who supposedly have the power to transform themselves into animals simply by wearing their pelts. Their Navajo name, *yee naaldlooshii*, means "with it, he goes on all fours." As if that's not alarming enough, Skinwalkers don't just walk around, playing at being animals—they use their new powers to attack, maim, and kill their human enemies. They can also take over people's bodies just by looking them in the eye. The only way to stop a Skinwalker, it is said, is to shoot it with a bullet dipped in white ash.

LYCANTHROPY

Feeling a bit bristly? Canine teeth getting bigger? Hungry? It could be a touch of lycanthropy. That's the scientific term for a medical condition that causes people to think they are turning into a wolf or other dangerous animal. It was common in medieval times, and cases still occur.

JERSEY DEVIL

In January 1909, a huge flying creature with bat-like wings, a reptilian body, and a horse's head and hooves scared the wits out of people in southern New Jersey. According to numerous reports, it swooped over buildings, attacked a bus, left hoofprints in the snow, and was fired at by police. Though it has been seen rarely since, a reward was offered for its capture in 1960 and many believe it still haunts the pinewoods.

ORANG PENDEK

Venture into the remote forests of Sumatra in Indonesia and you might bump into this alarming apelike human trudging through the trees.

Powerfully built and about 3 to 5 feet (1 to 1.5 m) tall, the Orang Pendek has long been part of local folklore but has also been sighted by scientists. Some say it's a member of a lost tribe of prehistoric humans, others an undiscovered species of ape.

Left: Jersey Devil.
Above right: Orang Pendek.

NANDI BEAR

It sounds kind of cute, doesn't it? But the Nandi Bear, a fierce meat-eating mammal said to inhabit the forests of western Kenya in Africa, doesn't just savage its victims, it also likes to feast on their brains—in fact one of its nicknames is "brain eater." The Nandi is unlikely to be a bear, since there are no native bears in Africa, but could be an overgrown form of hyena or, some say, a prehistoric carnivore previously thought to be extinct.

Cornish Owlman

Two young girls on vacation at the village of Mawnan in Cornwall, England, in April 1976, reported seeing a human-sized owl, with pointed ears, red eyes, and massive, pincer-like claws hovering over a church. They were so scared that their family decided to run home. Sightings occurred regularly over the next two years and have been reported occasionally since. The sightings coincided with some strange weather patterns that were going on (alternating heat waves and cold snaps) and an increase in the appearance of UFOs.

Beast of Bodmin Moor

Since 1983, more than 60 people claim to have seen a massive, black panther-like creature roaming Bodmin Moor in Cornwall, England. Many have heard its terrible howls drifting across the fields, and some claim their animals have been slain by it. Photographs and videos of the creature have been taken, but attempts by scientists and even soldiers to trap it have all failed.

Beast of Exmoor

A catlike creature is also said to roam Exmoor in Devon and Somerset, England, attacking sheep and cattle and posing a threat to walkers. It was first reported in the 1970s, but near-panic set in during the 1980s when a farmer claimed the beast had killed more than 100 of his sheep by ripping out their throats. Said to be as large as a panther, the beast has a grey or black coat and can leap over fences 6½ feet (2 m) high.

HYDRA

THE HYDRA is a many-headed serpent which is extremely dangerous and very hard to kill. The Hydra appears in tales of ancient Greece, but there are Hydra legends from Africa, too.

POISONOUS BREATH

The Hydra is like a huge water snake but has many heads, usually nine. One problem with a Hydra is that if you cut off one head, two more will grow in its place. Only one of its heads, if cut off, will actually kill the monster, and there's no way of telling which head that is. Another problem is that the Hydra has extremely poisonous breath, so you're likely to be dead before you've cut off more than one head anyway, just by letting the monster breathe on you.

HERCULES AND THE HYDRA

Hercules managed to kill a Hydra, but with help. He got his nephew Iolaus to scorch the stump of each head the moment Hercules had cut it off to stop the heads re-growing. The main head proved hard to hack off with a sword so Hercules had to smash it with a rock. Despite wearing cloths over their mouths, Hercules and Iolaus were almost killed by the poisonous breath before the Hydra was vanquished.

Lizard Man of Scape Ore Swamp

A strong humanlike creature with lizard skin.

The Lizard Man has been seen since the late 1980s around Scape Ore Swamp in North Carolina. It is tall, and mostly covered in greenish-black hair but with lizard-like skin on its hands, feet, and face. It has three toes on each foot and three fingers on each hand, is very strong, and has done serious damage to cars, which it seems to dislike.

Honey Island Swamp Monster

An ape-man of the Louisana swamps.

This monster has been sighted since the 1960s. It's a humanlike creature, roughly 6½ feet (2 m) tall, with long grayish hair and red eyes. It smells disgusting, and its footprints have only four toes. Honey Island Swamp is a very wild area along the Pearl River in Louisiana. At least 13 people there have claimed to have seen the monster, and, apparently, there are others who prefer not to say in public if they've seen it or not, but privately admit that they have met "the thing," as it's locally known.

Lizard Man of Scape Ore Swamp

MUMMY

MUMMY

FACT OR FICTION: Mummified bodies are fact, but the idea of monstrous mummies rising from the dead and attacking people is purely fiction.

DESCRIPTION: A mummy is always wrapped in linen bandages. Usually these are dirty, tattered, and torn, and sometimes unravel, revealing the mummy's body and rotting flesh.

WHERE THEY LIVE: The most famous real mummies are from Egypt, but there are also mummies in South America, China, New Guinea, Australia, and Europe.

POWERS: A mummy is tremendously strong and resistant to bullets, knives, sticks, and stones—mainly because it's already dead. It can possess the mind or body of a living person.

WEAKNESSES: Can't resist fire, so burning a mummy is the best way to get rid of one. Some ancient spells can be effective too.

OTHER CHARACTERISTICS: Dead mummies can be brought to life by conducting a ritual, or reciting a spell or incantation.

WRAPPED IN TATTERED BANDAGES, the mummy rises from its ancient Egyptian tomb to haunt, terrify, and sometimes kill people. It may seek revenge against those who disturbed it or against the descendants of its ancient enemies. It may try to raise a long-lost loved one from the dead, while murdering anyone who gets in its way.

PRESERVING THE DEAD

Mummification is the process of treating, or embalming, a dead body so that it will not rot. It was most famously practiced by the ancient Egyptians, but was used in other parts of the world, too. Animals can also be mummified.

In ancient Egypt, the process involved covering the body in salt to dry it out, then rubbing the skin with oils or resin to keep it flexible. The body was then stuffed with a filling, such as sand or sawdust, and wrapped in linen bandages to stop the air getting into it. Finally, the corpse was sealed inside a strong coffin, or sarcophagus, and placed within a tomb. The dry desert air would also help preserve the body.

A SMALL BAG OF MUMMY, PLEASE

People in the Middle Ages believed that mummies contained a tarlike substance called bitumen, which they thought could heal a variety of diseases. (The word "mummy" actually comes from the Arabic mumiyah, meaning "bitumen.") As a result, many ancient Egyptian corpses were ground up into a powder called "mummy" that was sold all over Europe. When traders ran out of Egyptian mummies, they sneakily started using the bodies of criminals. This practice continued until the eighteenth century.

CURSE OF THE MUMMY

From ancient times, it was said that anyone who opened the tomb of a pharaoh would suffer bad luck forever after, and a number of tombs actually contained written warnings, such as "Cursed be those who disturb the rest of a Pharaoh." From the eighteenth century onwards, several explorers and archaeologists reported bad things happening to them after entering tombs, including illnesses, accidents, and mummies haunting their dreams.

Soon after a British expedition led by Howard Carter opened the tomb of Egyptian pharaoh Tutankhamen in 1922, several members of the party were struck by misfortune. The expedition's sponsor, Lord Carnarvon, got a mosquito bite on his left cheek and died of blood poisoning— spookily, the body of Tutankhamen was said to have a wound in the same place. Others also died of fevers or blood diseases, were murdered, or committed suicide.

A story even circulated that on the day Carter entered the tomb his house was broken into and his canary eaten by a cobra —the symbol of ancient Egyptian rulers. Carter, however, lived for another 17 years, dying at the age of 64.

Below: Howard Carter examining the mummy of King Tutankhamen in 1922.

Below: Mummified bodies from the Capuchin Catacombs in Palermo, Italy.

THE UNDEAD

Mummies are often considered to be "undead" in their tomb. Some people attempt to bring them back to life to serve them as their own personal monster to fight off enemies. A mummy may be brought back to life by performing a ritual or reciting an ancient spell. Sometimes tomb robbers or archaeologists do this unwittingly by reading out inscriptions they find in a tomb. Even before they have finished speaking, the sarcophagus starts to open and a bandaged hand reaches out and then they are in trouble! However, if you're lucky, as soon as the mummy is exposed to air, it may disintegrate.

If you unleash a mummy by mistake and don't know what you're doing, controlling it can be challenging. Reburying it might work if you can first immobilize it, but there's no guarantee that it won't be dug up again later. Sometimes reciting another spell will cause a mummy to become mortal and quickly age and die. But burning it to ashes is usually a swifter and surer way.

BIGFOOT

A KIND OF APE-MAN seen in remote areas of North America. Some say he looks like a tall, light-brown gorilla but that he stands upright like a human and makes a strange whistling noise. He is very shy, so it is mostly only Bigfoot's giant footsteps in the snow that are seen by people.

BIGFOOT

OTHER NAMES: Sasquatch.

FACT OR FICTION: Most people think that Bigfoot is fact, since footprints have been found. Some famous scientists believe in its existence.

DESCRIPTION: Like a tall, hairy gorilla or ape-man, but standing upright like a human. Some say Bigfoot has short, light-colored fur or hair all over while other say dark or red hair. Around 6 to 10 feet (2 to 3 m) tall and probably weighs more than 500 pounds (230 kg).

WHERE THEY LIVE: Remote forest areas of the Pacific Northwest region of North America in Canada and the United States. Bigfoot is thought to be nocturnal.

POWERS: Physically huge and powerfully built, so it can easily catch and overpower large animals or humans.

WEAKNESSES: Does not like bright lights or daylight. Shy of humans.

DIET: An omnivore, meaning that it eats both meat and plants.

SIGHTINGS OF BIGFOOT

The first reported Bigfoot was seen in the Pacific Northwest of North America. Hunters reported meeting a very tall, hairy figure in the mountains, looking like a light-brown gorilla but standing upright like a human. The creature was shy, and when anyone approached, it would disappear into the forest. Its footprints were seen in the soft mud along rivers and were up to 2 feet (60 cm) long. It made a strange whistling noise. The Native American Lummi Nation had many stories about this creature, and it was also known as the Sasquatch, based on the name it had amongst the First Nation people over the border in Canada.

Later, people in the Great Lakes area and in some southeastern states began saying that they had seen a Bigfoot in their own part of the country. There were numerous sightings in California, and reports have come from many parts of the United States over the years.

Bigfoot mostly seems to be wary of people and not dangerous, unless you do something to harm it. However, some people believe that seeing it will bring extremely bad luck. (See also Yeti on page 20.)

ATTACK OF THE BIGFOOT

In 1924, five men mining for gold in the wild Mount St. Helens area of Washington state saw huge footprints and heard strange whistling sounds which seemed to call and answer each other across the valley. As they were coming back to the cabin, two of the men saw a Bigfoot some distance away. They fired their rifles at it, and were sure they had wounded it before it disappeared into the forest. That night, the men awoke from their sleep in terror. The cabin was being attacked by a group of Bigfoot. One got its huge arm through a gap in the wall and tried to grab an axe that was hanging there, but the miners shot at its hand and it pulled its arm back. Luckily, the cabin was strongly built and the Bigfoot weren't able to get in.

Hunters in the snow come across the terrifying sight of Bigfoot.

YETI

A MYSTERIOUS apelike creature of the Himalayas, also known as the Abominable Snowman. It is a large, two-legged creature covered in long hair. Like Bigfoot it is tall and walks like a human, rather than an ape, and leaves large footprints.

YETI

OTHER NAMES: Abominable Snowman.

FACT OR FICTION: Some people believe it is fact, especially people living in the Himalayas, but most scientists think the Yeti is fiction.

DESCRIPTION: An apelike creature covered in long hair, which walks on two legs like a human.

WHERE THEY LIVE: Mountains in the Himalayan region of Nepal in Asia.

POWERS: Strong and physically powerful. It may only attack to protect itself.

WEAKNESSES: Shy of humans, so rarely seen.

DIET: Unknown.

ABOMINABLE FOOTPRINTS

The main evidence for the Yeti, or Abominable Snowman, is the large footprints in the snow, which have been seen quite often. Some scientists believe that in certain weather conditions, footprints will spread in snow and give the impression of a much larger foot than they were actually made by. So, they think the prints could be made by a bear or even a fox.

However, Yeti have been seen by local Tibetan people. For example, one girl was herding yaks when a Yeti appeared and grabbed her. Luckily, it let her go when she screamed loudly, but the monster killed two of her yaks.

Several expeditions have gone to the Himalayas trying to find evidence of Yeti, but without success. All the same, many people believe that Yeti do exist.

SAVED BY A YETI

In 1938, Captain d'Auvergne, who was the Curator of the Victoria Memorial in Calcutta (Kolkata), India, and a highly respected scholar, was traveling alone in the Himalayas. He became ill with snow-blindness—a condition resulting from over-exposure of the eyes to ultraviolet light; it causes sudden loss of sight and acute pain. He wandered blindly in the mountains until he was close to dying from exposure to the elements.

Then, suddenly, he was rescued by someone, carried to a cave, and fed. As his sight gradually returned, he saw that his rescuer was a tall and hairy Yeti, which gently nursed him back to health until he was well enough to go home.

OTHER YETI-LIKE CREATURES

There are similar stories told all over the world of hairy ape-men living in the wilderness. Most of these creatures are from mountainous areas.

Yeti-type creatures have also been seen in Queensland, Victoria, and New South Wales, Australia. In the Basque country of northern Spain, a similar creature is known as the Basajaun. In Vietnam, Laos, and Borneo, there is a creature called the Batutut, and, in South America, there is one is called the Maricoxi. For something that supposedly doesn't exist, it turns up in a lot of places!

Right: A preserved skull, said to be that of the Yeti, is on display at a monastery near Mount Everest.

WILD MAN

FABLED IN MANY PARTS of Europe in particular, the Wild Man is a huge humanlike creature covered in thick hair who lives in dense forests. He is sometimes referred to as the Wodewose, an Old English term meaning "wild person of the woods."

WILD AND HAIRY

Wild Men seek out the most inaccessible forest realms, living on nuts, berries, and the raw flesh of animals, and sometimes sleeping in caves. They have no desire to mix with normal humans and can become violent if they encounter them—occasionally they even attack and eat people. Especially savage are the Wild Men of the Alps, who have legs as thick as tree trunks and will immediately tear to pieces anybody who has the misfortune to wander into their domain.

Forest beings like the Wild Man are described in ancient literature. The Greek historian Herodotus claimed to have seen them in North Africa in the fifth century BC, and Greek myths include similar figures such as the Silvanus, the wild protector of the woods, who occasionally punished humans. In the Middle Ages, the Wild Man became a famous figure of folklore in Europe and was often depicted in paintings, coats of arms, and carved into the architecture of great buildings, such as Canterbury Cathedral in England.

CHINESE WILDMAN

Many travelers roaming the forested hills of the Hubei region of central China have had the fright of their lives when coming upon the Chinese Wildman, also known as the Yeren or Man-Monkey. Described as being 9 feet (2.7 m) tall, powerfully built, and covered in reddish hair, he is thought by some to be a Chinese ogre, though others say he might be a species of humanlike ape or a giant orangutan.

MO-MO

Also known as the Missouri monster, Mo-mo was first seen in woods near the town of Louisiana, Missouri, in 1972, by two girls on a picnic and later sighted repeatedly in the region. A hairy, humanlike ape more than 6½ feet (2 m) tall, it is thought to feed on dogs and other animals. Most people are struck by its foul smell—"worse than a family of skunks," said the first witnesses.

GOATMAN

In Prince George's County, Maryland, this frightening beast with the legs and hooves of a goat and the upper body of a human—and some say horns and pointed ears—is said to roam the countryside attacking cars with an axe. One theory is that he was formerly a scientist working in a nearby research laboratory whose experiment went disastrously wrong, turning him into the Goatman.

MOKÉLE-MBÊMBE

The Mokéle-Mbêmbe is said to live in the swamps of the Congo River in Africa. It's a big greyish-creature with a long neck, a small head, and a long tail. Some say that it looks like a dinosaur. It's not known to be dangerous, but it would probably be alarming if you met it suddenly. It may be a living reptile—some type of lizard, or even a dinosaur which has somehow survived—or it may be a kind of river spirit.

BEHEMOTH

The Behemoth is an enormous swamp-dwelling monster mentioned in the Bible (Book of Job, Chapter 40). Not much is known about it except that it is very, very large. It may be like a hippopotamus, only much bigger. People often refer to huge things today as "Behemoths."

Top: Behemoth is a massive hippopotamus-like creature that is mentioned in the Bible.

MANTICORE

The Manticore is a terrifying man-eating monster from ancient Persia and India.

This legendary monster is famous for devouring every part of its victims, including their clothing and any luggage they might be carrying. If you are eaten by a Manticore, there will be nothing left behind at all, not even your shoelaces!

The Manticore lives in jungles and swampy areas in India and Iran. It has the body and legs of a lion, the head of a man with piercing blue eyes, three rows of teeth, and a long tail with detachable poisonous spines at the end. As the monster waves its tail angrily, the deadly spines whiz through the air toward you. If they hit you, they will probably kill you. The Manticore can run extremely fast and has an ear-splittingly loud voice that can paralyze victims with fear, giving it plenty of time to pounce.

There's not much chance of survival if you do meet a Manticore. If you can stay calm, it may be possible to play for time by asking it a very clever riddle, but it will have heard most of the good ones since it's been around for a very long time.

STYMPHALIAN BIRDS

The mythical hero Hercules had to get rid of the ferocious and poisonous birds that were living in the swampy Lake Stymphalia. These birds had metal beaks and feathers. They could pull out their feathers and throw them like poison darts. They ate people as well as crops and fruit, and terrorized the neighborhood. Hercules shot most of them with arrows, after which the remaining birds moved elsewhere.

TALOS

TALOS was a bronze giant of ancient Greek myth who lived on the island of Crete. His job was to guard the princess Europa who lived on the island and to drive off any invaders or pirates. He had molten lead in his single vein.

BRONZE GIANT

The giant Talos, from ancient Greek mythology, was made entirely of bronze. He may have been a living giant, but was more likely a kind of animated statue or robot. In some stories, he had bronze wings. Talos was fierce and dangerous, and was the guardian of the island of Crete. He walked or flew all the way around the coast of the island three times every day, watching for pirates or other invaders. If any ship came near, he would throw huge rocks at it. He was put on Crete to guard the princess Europa, who had been taken to the island by Zeus, the king of the gods. Zeus was in love with Europa and had abducted her and placed her on this island.

Talos's bronze body came in useful at times. He could jump into a fire and heat himself until he was red hot, so that he could then clasp his enemies in a murderous, scorching hug. He was finally destroyed by the enchantress Medea, who first hypnotized him with the help of some evil spirits. She then removed a plug from his ankle that allowed the liquid metal, which he had instead of blood, to run out onto the ground. The bronze giant bled to death.

CYCLOPS

A CYCLOPS is an extremely strong and bad-tempered giant of ancient Greek and Roman legend, who only had one terrifying eye in the middle of his forehead. The word "cyclops" probably means "round eye."

ONE-EYED MONSTERS

The Cyclopes were legendary giants. Each Cyclops had only one eye in the middle of his forehead. Cyclopes lived a very long time, were immensely strong even for giants, and were well known for their terrible tempers and generally grouchy dispositions.

Cyclopes were often blacksmiths, but the most famous Cyclops is Polyphemus, who was a shepherd and lived on an island with his own herd of giant sheep. He captured the great Greek traveler Odysseus (from Homer's epic tale, *The Odyssey*) and his companions when they landed on the island and wandered into his cave by accident.

To the captive travelers' horror, Polyphemus began killing and eating them, two for each meal, and no amount of persuasion would change his intention to eat them all. Finally, Odysseus managed to trick Polyphemus into getting very drunk, and then blinded his eye using a stick of wood. But even blind, Polyphemus was dangerous, and the Greeks only escaped him by hiding among his big sheep when he let the flock out in the morning.

The enraged and blinded Polyphemus called on Poseidon, the sea god, for revenge, and Poseidon sent wild storms to threaten Odysseus and his companions as they continued their voyage.

GLOSSARY

Archeologist: a scientist that studies the life, tools, monuments, and remains left by ancient peoples

Bitumen: a tar-like substance used to make some mummies

Carnivore: a meat-eating animal

Curator: a person in charge of a museum or zoo

Descendant: one that comes from an earlier and similar individual

Embalm: to treat a dead body with special preparations in order to preserve it from decay

Incantation: a series of words used to produce a magic spell

Lycanthropy: the scientific term for a medical condition that causes people to think they are turning into a wolf or other dangerous animal

Medieval times: the Middle Ages

Middle Ages: the period of European history from about A.D. 500 to about 1500

Mythology: a collection of myths dealing with the gods/goddesses of a particular people

Navajo: a member of an American Indian people of northern New Mexico and Arizona

Nocturnal: active at night

Ointment: a liquid medicine for use on the skin

Old English: the language of the English people before about 1100

Omnivore: an animal that eats meat and plants

Pelt: an unfinished skin with its hair, wool, or fur

Pharaoh: a ruler of ancient Egypt

Prehistoric: of, relating to, or existing in the time before written history

Resin: an oil used during the process of mummification

Sarcophagus: a stone coffin

INDEX

Please visit our website, www.garethstevens.com. For a free color catalog of all our high-quality books, call toll free 1-800-542-2595 or fax 1-877-542-2596.

Library of Congress Cataloging-in-Publication Data

Cox, Barbara.
Maniacal monsters and bizarre beasts / by Barbara Cox and Scott Forbes.
  p. cm. — (Creepy chronicles)
Includes index.
ISBN 978-1-4824-0239-1 (pbk.)
ISBN 978-1-4824-0240-7 (6-pack)
ISBN 978-1-4824-0236-0 (library binding)
1. Monsters — Juvenile literature. 2. Supernatural — Juvenile literature. I. Title.
GR825.C69 2014
001.944—dc23

First Edition

Published in 2014 by
Gareth Stevens Publishing
111 East 14th Street, Suite 349
New York, NY 10003

© 2014 Red Lemon Press Limited

Produced for Gareth Stevens by Red Lemon Press Limited
Concept and Project Manager: Ariana Klepac
Designer: Emilia Toia
Design Assistant: Haylee Bruce
Picture Researcher: Ariana Klepac
Text: Scott Forbes (Forest, Castle, Desert), Barbara Cox (all other text)
Indexer: Trevor Matthews

Images: Every effort has been made to trace and contact the copyright holders prior to publication. If notified, the publisher undertakes to rectify any errors or omissions at the earliest opportunity.

Alamy: 16 t
Bridgeman Art Library: 2 tl and b, 3 tr, 8 t, 10 tr in box, 12 t, 14 tl,
17 t and b, 18 c, 18–19 background, 19 br, 20–21 background,
21 tr in box, 22 tl, 24 t, 27 tr.
Getty Images: 16 b in box, 21 br.
iStockphoto: other images as follows:
cross stitches 7, 11, 14, 16, 17; grunge borders 15, 19, 21; hands 15, 19, 21, 27; scratches 6, 7, 8, 9;
stick borders 14, 18, 20; werewolf cover and 7.
Martin Hargreaves: 13 r, 26 tl.
Shutterstock: all other images

KEY: t = top, b = bottom, l = left, r = right, c = center

Printed in the United States of America

CPSIA compliance information: Batch #CW14GS; For further information contact Gareth Stevens, New York, New York at 1-800-542-2595.

Gareth Stevens
Publishing